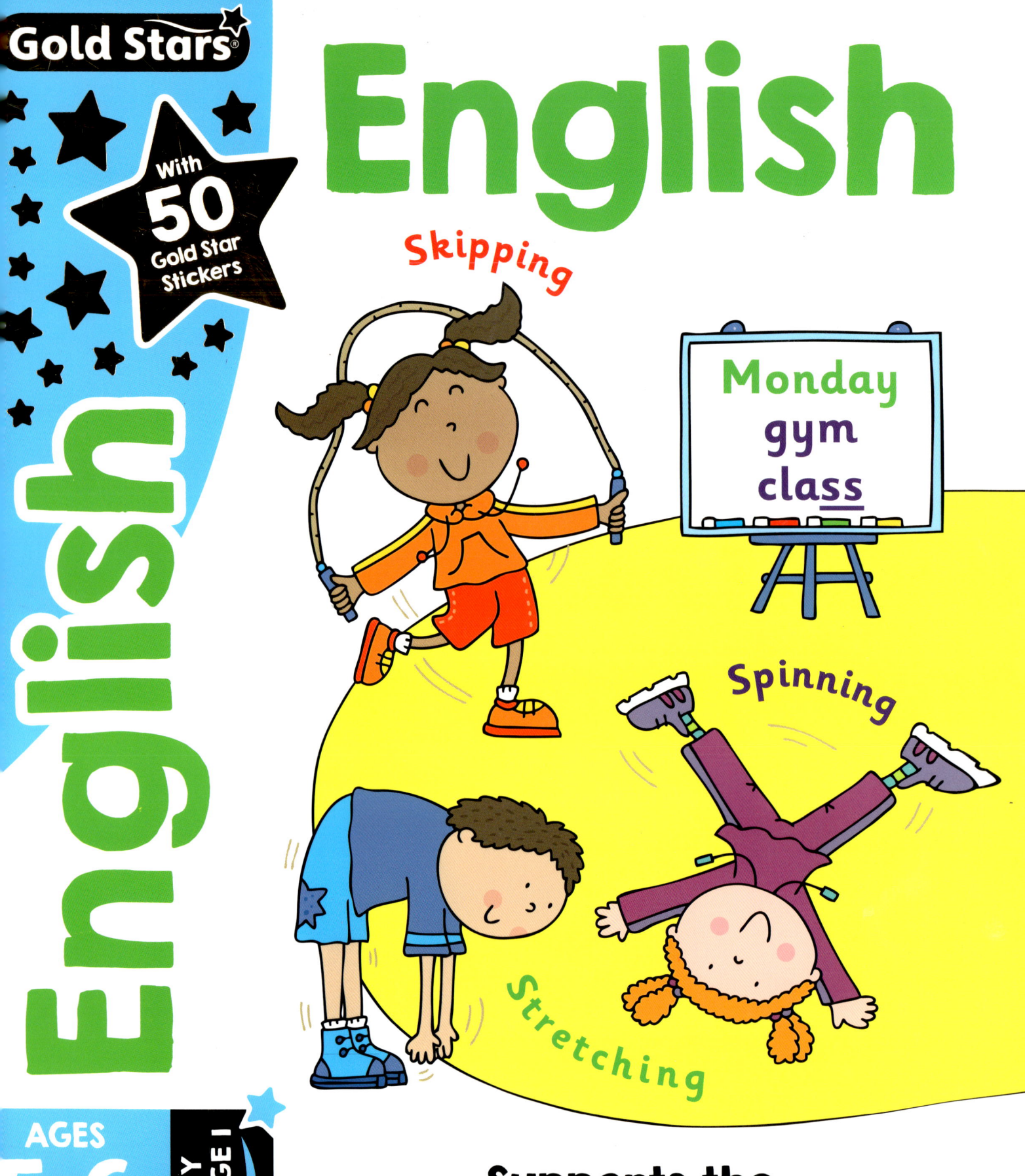

# Contents

| | | | |
|---|---|---|---|
| All about me | 4 | Little words | 19 |
| Labels | 5 | Find the right word | 20 |
| Middle vowel sounds | 6 | Making sentences | 21 |
| Odd one out | 8 | Alphabetical order | 22 |
| Yes or no? | 9 | Days of the week | 23 |
| Writing labels | 10 | Find your way | 24 |
| The alphabet | 11 | Telephone numbers | 25 |
| Consonant blends | 12 | Animal dictionary | 26 |
| Quick quiz | 14 | Reading an index | 27 |
| Read and draw | 15 | Making word banks | 28 |
| The Enormous Turnip | 16 | Words and sentences | 30 |
| How does it end? | 17 | Find the rhymes | 31 |
| Alphabetical order | 18 | Answers | 32 |

# All about me

Write in the missing words.

My name is _____.

I am _____ years old.

I live at _____

_____

_____.

My school is called _____.

My favourite animal is _____.

My favourite sport is _____.

4

Note for parent: In this activity your child is reading and writing and providing information. Ask them to point out the capital letters and full stops.

# Labels

Draw yourself in the box.
Read the words and draw a line to the right part.

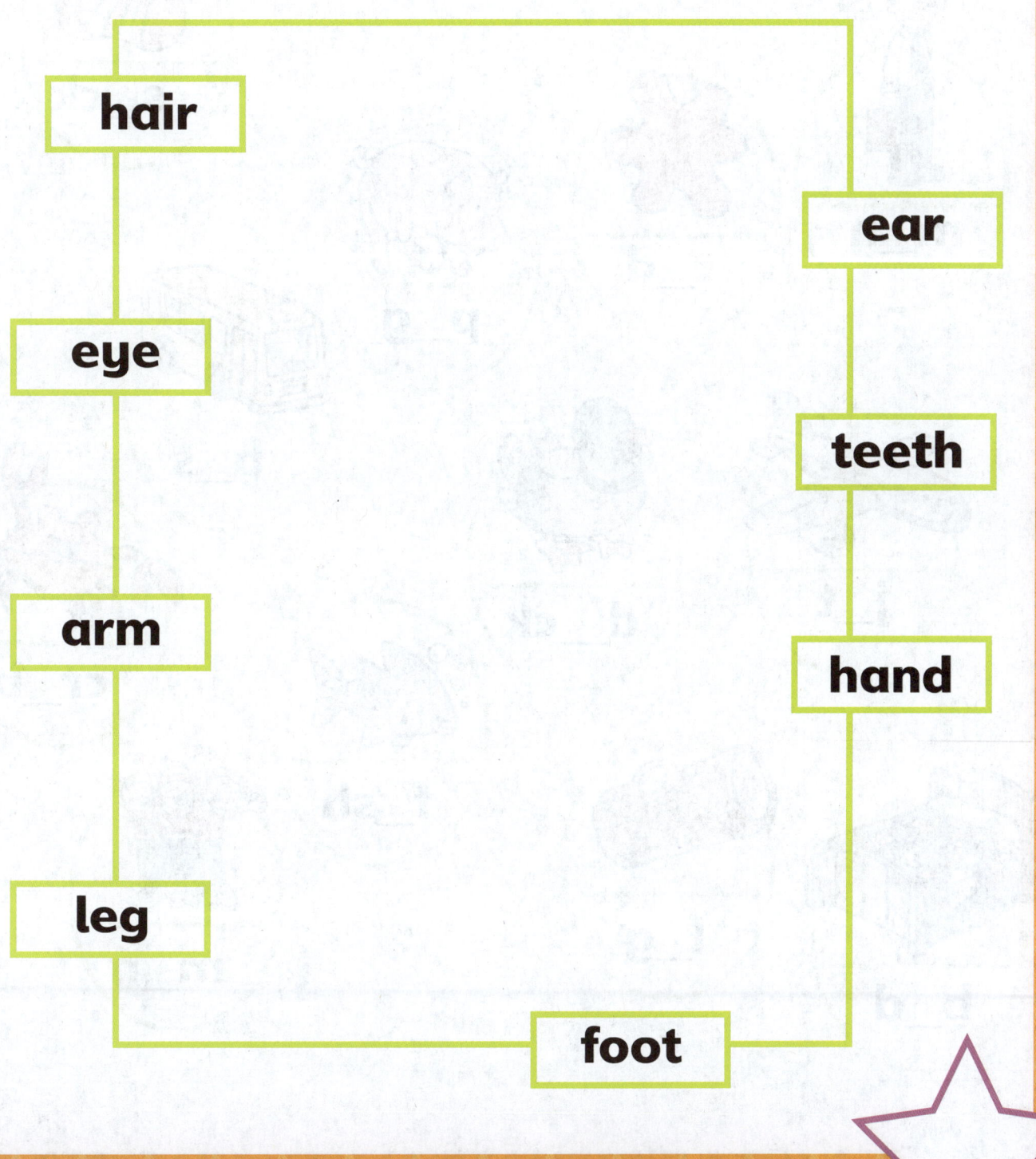

# Middle vowel sounds

Use the vowels **a, e, i, o** or **u** to complete the words below.

m_n
r_d
p_g
s_ck
j_t
d_ck
b_s
cr_b
b_d
l_g
f_sh
m_n

Join the pictures that have the same middle sounds – **a, e, i, o** or **u**.

# Odd one out

Cross out the picture in each row that does not belong.

# Yes or no?

Look at the picture. Read the sentences and write **yes** or **no** next to each one.

The teacher is under the table. \_\_\_\_\_
The girl is reading a book. \_\_\_\_\_
The boy is painting the door. \_\_\_\_\_
The teacher is looking at the girl. \_\_\_\_\_
The cat is reading a book. \_\_\_\_\_
The boy has got a brush. \_\_\_\_\_
The hamster is on its cage. \_\_\_\_\_

Note for parent: This activity helps your child begin to understand simple comprehension, looking for picture and word clues to help them find their answers.

# Writing labels

Read these words:

**ball   boy   girl   man   car   tree**

Now choose a word to write in each box, to label the picture.

Note for parent: This activity gives practice with reading words and placing them in the correct context.

# The alphabet

Write in the missing letters. Some are capital letters and some are lower-case ones.
Draw your own pictures in the empty squares.

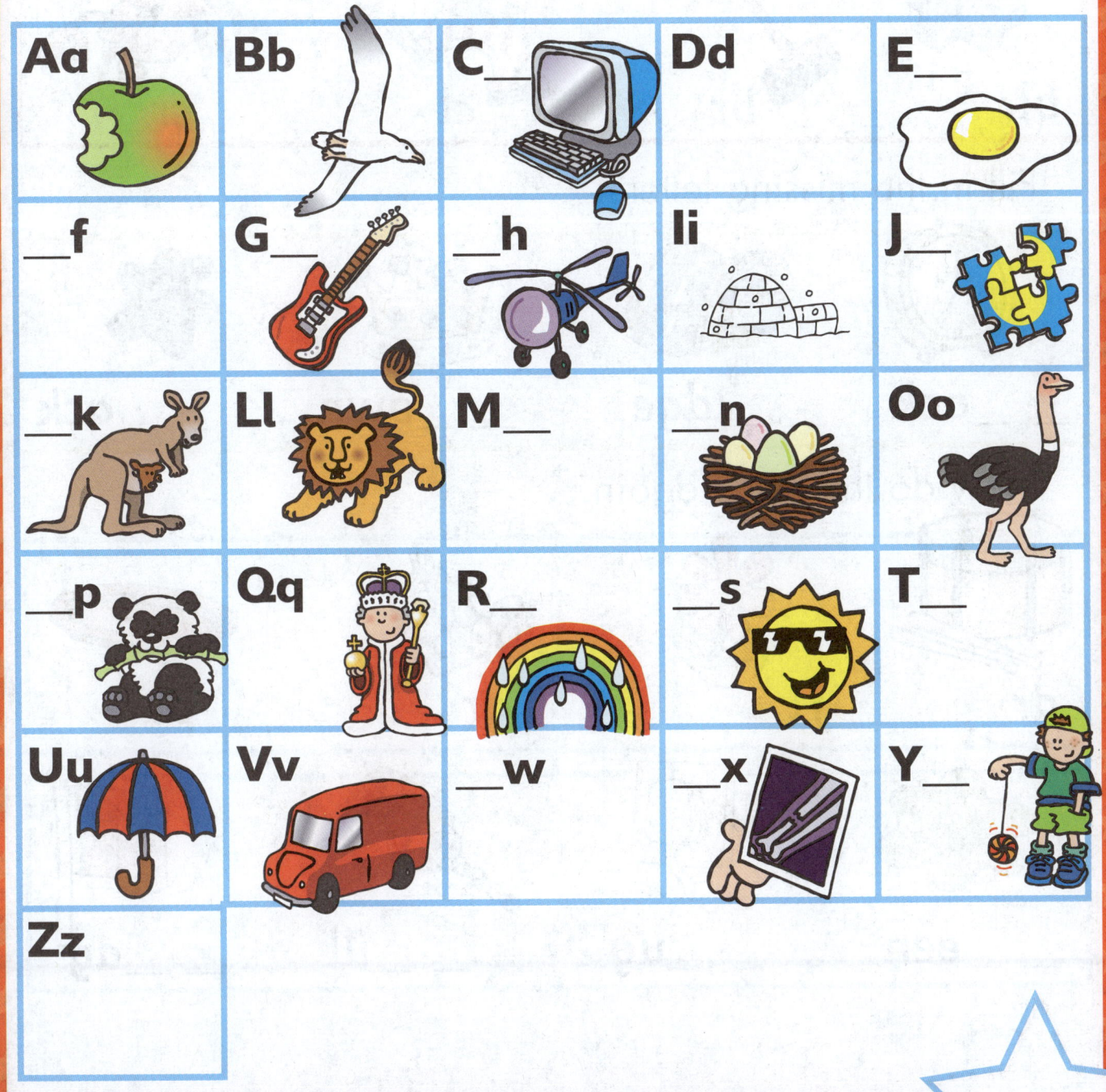

# Consonant blends

Look at these pictures and say each beginning sound.

**bl**   **br**  **cl**   **cr**

Fill in the missing letters.

_ _ock    _ _idge    _ _own    _ _ack

Now do the same again.

**dr**    **fl**    **gr**    **pl**

_ _een    _ _ug    _ _ill    _ _ag

Look at the first picture in each row.
Tick the other pictures in the same row that start in the same way.

Note for parent: This activity helps your child to identify and use 12 consonant blends at the beginning of words.

# Quick quiz

Join each sound to a picture. Say the picture names out loud to help you.

# Read and draw

Read the sentences and finish the picture.

Draw a tree <u>by</u> the river.
Draw a boat going <u>under</u> the bridge.
Draw a duck <u>on</u> the river.
Draw a car going <u>over</u> the bridge.
Draw a sun <u>up</u> in the sky.

Note for parent: This activity helps children to learn positional words such as by, under, on, over and up.

# The Enormous Turnip

Look at the pictures. Read the sentences.
Match each sentence to the correct picture.

Everyone fell over and the turnip came out. __

The farmer saw an enormous turnip. __

Everyone tried to pull up the turnip. __

The farmer tried to pull up the turnip. __

Note for parent: This activity gives your child practice in sequencing and making sense of a simple story.

# Alphabetical order

a b c d e f g h i j k l m n o p q r s t u v w x y z

Write the beginning sound of each picture. Then put the three letters in each row in alphabetical order.

# Little words

Find each little word in one of the big words and then join them with a line.

**or**

**us**

**an**

**all**

**am**

**in**

**at**

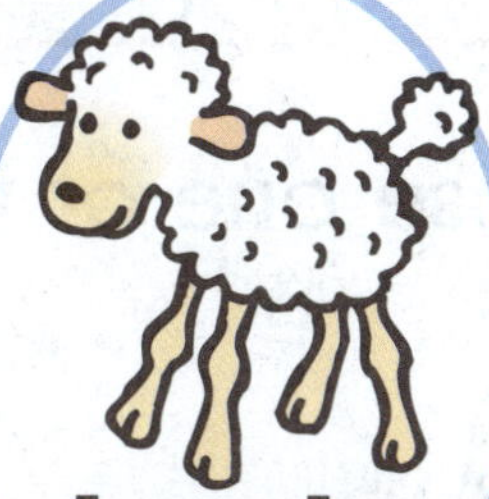

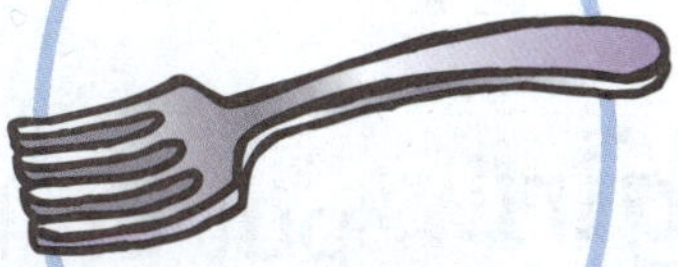

**lamb**

**fork**

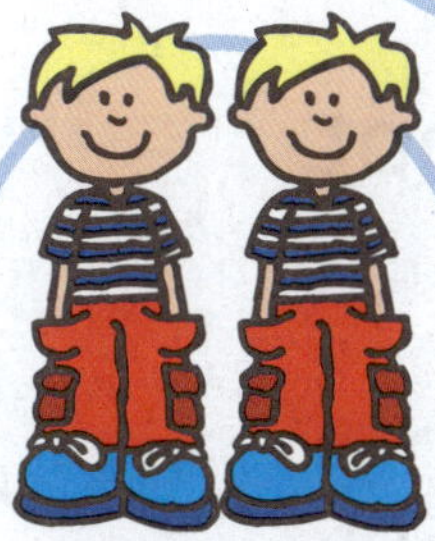

**twins**

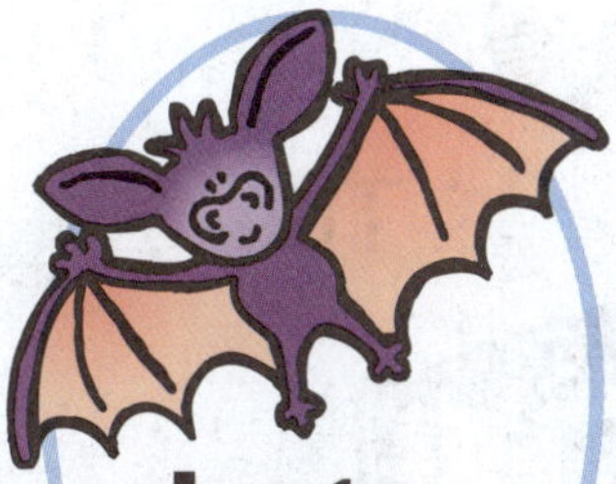

**bat**

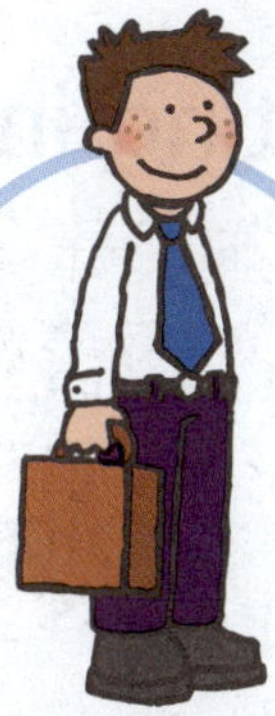

**man**

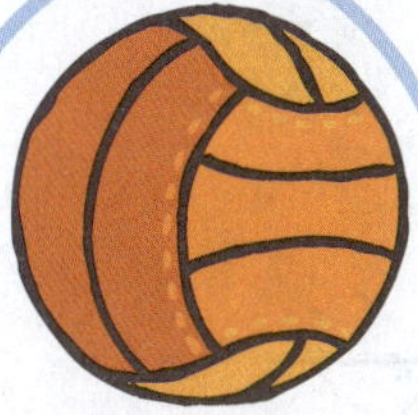

**ball**

**bus**

How many of the little words can you read? _____

Note for parent: Your child will use these smaller words regularly so it's good to practise reading them.

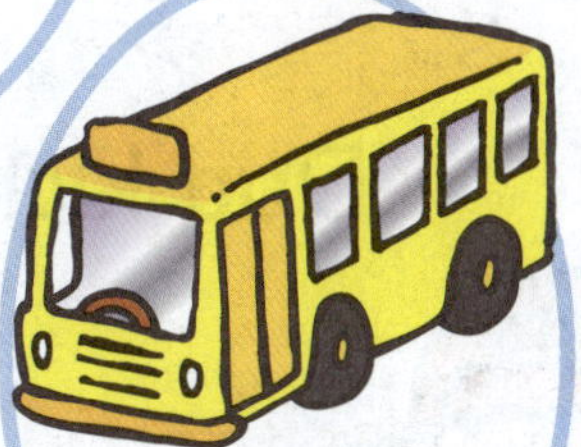

# Find the right word

| sun | bed | boy | ball | girl | tree |

Choose one of these words to write in each sentence.

A little __girl__ put on her dress.

The _____ was hot.

I like getting into my _____ to go to sleep.

I can see a bird's nest in the _____ .

Dad kicked the _____ .

A little _____ put on his football boots.

# Making sentences

These sentences are all muddled. Write them in the right order and then finish each one with a full stop . or a question mark ?

is time What the

_____

fruit I to like eat

_____

do go school When I to

_____

car going The was fast

_____

up Who the with went Jill hill

_____

on lap The likes sit to my cat

_____

How many capital letters can you count?____

# Alphabetical order

Look at the names and then write them in the register in the correct order. Remember to use capital letters.

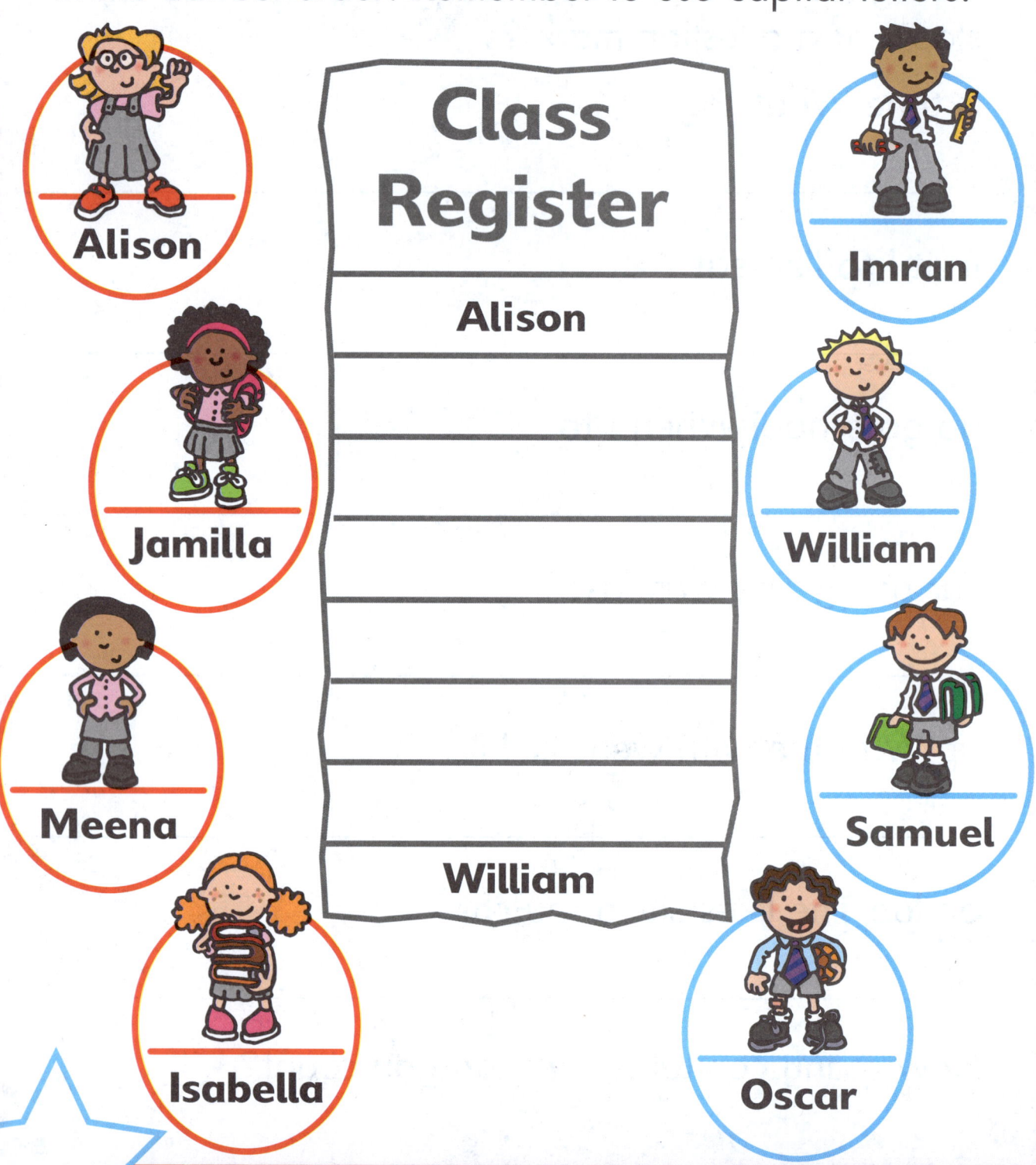

# Days of the week

Look at the pictures. Read the questions and then write the correct day. Remember the capital letters.

**Monday**

When does Clare go trampolining? _____

When does Clare watch television? _____

**Friday**

When does Jack go to the library? _____

**Tuesday**

When does Clare go shopping? _____

**Saturday**

When does Jack wash the car? _____

**Wednesday**

When does Clare take the dog out? _____

**Sunday**

When does Jack play football? _____

**Thursday**

Note for parent: This activity helps your child to use their comprehension skills as well as learn to write the days of the week.

# Find your way

Read these instructions. Draw the correct way from the house to the school.

Start at ✗.

Walk down the path and turn out of the gate.

Turn right after the trees.

Walk along the path to the traffic lights.

Go over the zebra crossing.

Turn right and then turn left into **School Road**.

Go past the fence and turn left through the school gate.

# Telephone numbers

Use this telephone directory to answer the questions at the bottom of the page.

| | | | |
|---|---|---|---|
| *Mr Anderson* | 9802 | *Mr Mead* | 9980 |
| *Mr Caswell* | 9146 | *Miss Palmer* | 9544 |
| *Mrs Depster* | 9829 | *Mr Shah* | 9827 |
| *Miss Heelan* | 9026 | *Mrs Todd* | 9412 |
| *Ms Kamara* | 9530 | *Ms Walker* | 9361 |

What is Mr Shah's number? _____

What is Miss Heelan's number? _____

What is Mr Caswell's number? _____

What is Miss Palmer's number? _____

Whose number is 9361? _____

Whose number is 9802? _____

Whose number is 9412? _____

Whose number is 9829? _____

Do you know your own telephone number at home? _____

# Animal dictionary

Match each word to the correct meaning.
Draw a line to join them.

**elephant**

A large animal that can jump very well. It carries its young in a pouch. It comes from Australia.

**kangaroo**

A small animal with long arms and feet that it uses like hands. It lives in jungles.

**monkey**

A large animal with a long trunk and ivory tusks. It lives in Africa and Asia.

**panda**

An animal like a horse with black and white stripes. It lives in Africa.

**zebra**

A black and white animal like a bear. It lives in China.

# Reading an index

Use the index below to answer the questions at the bottom of the page.

## Index

| | | | |
|---|---|---|---|
| Apes | 10 | Kangaroos | 20 |
| Bears | 8 | Monkeys | 6 |
| Chimpanzees | 14 | Penguins | 28 |
| Crocodiles | 22 | Sharks | 4 |
| Dolphins | 26 | Turtles | 12 |
| Giraffes | 18 | Whales | 16 |

Page 18 is about _____

Page 28 is about _____

Page 16 is about _____

Page 8 is about _____

Page 12 is about _____

Apes are on page _____

Sharks are on page _____

Kangaroos are on page _____

Giraffes are on page _____

Chimpanzees are on page _____

Which page would you like to read? _____

Why? _____

Note for parent: Using an index is an important skill for your child to learn.

# Making word banks

Write the words in the correct lists.

| Things I eat | Things I see on wheels |
|---|---|
|  |  |

sandwich

van

egg

train

apple

bicycle

car

banana

bus

grapes

28

Write the words in the correct lists.

| Things I use in the kitchen | Things I use in the garden |
|---|---|

spade

pan

knife

wheelbarrow

frying pan

watering can

spoon

fork

food processor

lawnmower

Note for parent: Word banks are useful for your child to keep and use for independent writing.

29

# Words and sentences

Make two more words by adding one letter.

**ball**  __all  __all

Write a sentence with each of the two words you have made.

1._____

2._____

Now do the same again with these words.

**man**  ___an  ___an

**hat**  ___at  ___at

1._____

2._____

1._____

2._____

30

Note for parent: As well as spelling simple words, this activity encourages your child's independent writing skills.

# Find the rhymes

Colour in blue the words that rhyme with **take**.
Colour in green the words that rhyme with **ball**.
Colour in red the words that rhyme with **shell**.
Colour in yellow the words that rhyme with **pin**.

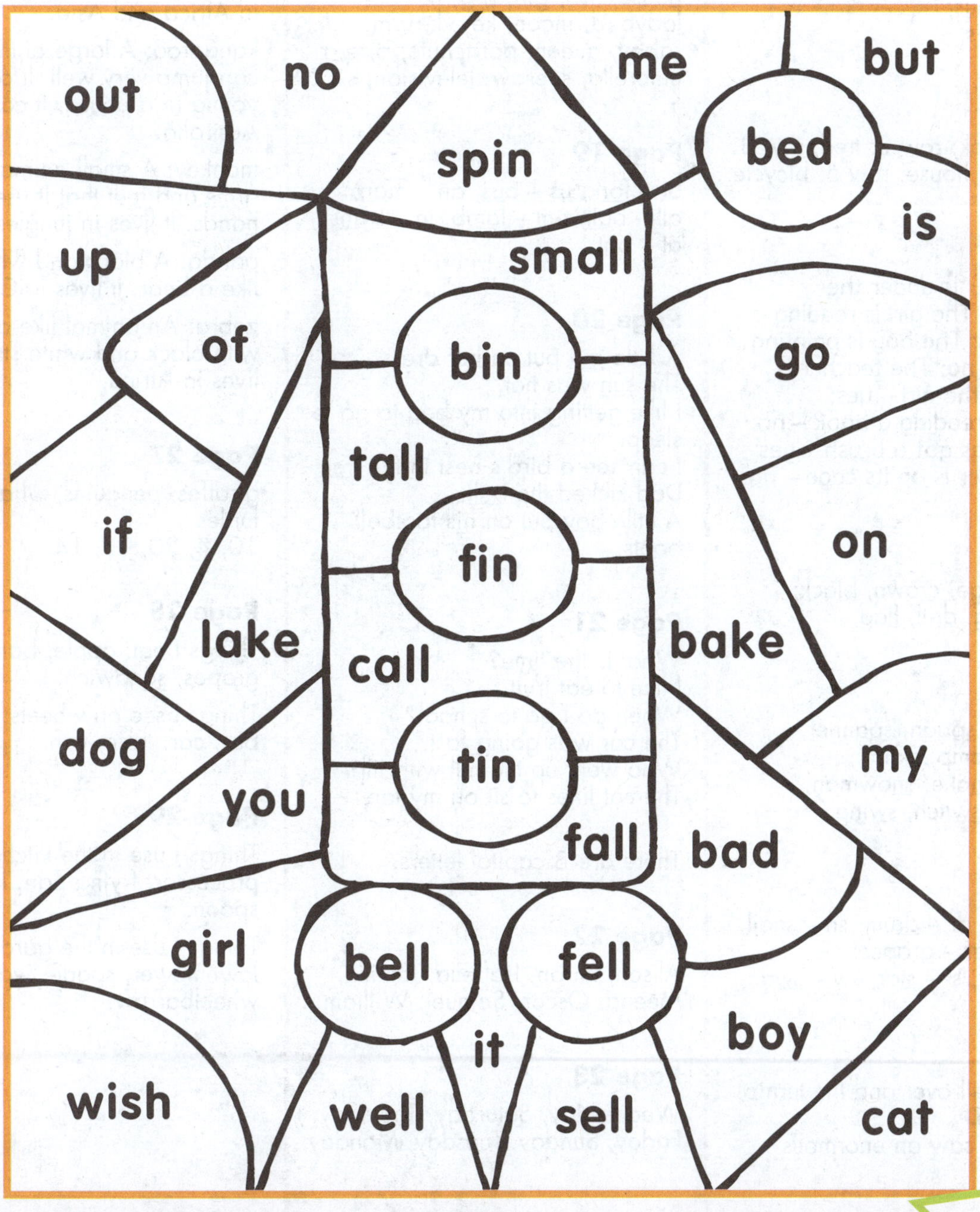

# Answers

**Page 6**

m<u>a</u>n, r<u>e</u>d, p<u>i</u>g, s<u>o</u>ck, j<u>e</u>t, d<u>u</u>ck, b<u>u</u>s, b<u>e</u>d, l<u>o</u>g, f<u>i</u>sh, cr<u>a</u>b, m<u>e</u>n.

**Page 7**

<u>d</u>og, <u>f</u>ox, <u>l</u>og;
<u>h</u>at, <u>b</u>at, <u>f</u>an;
<u>b</u>ell, <u>w</u>eb, <u>p</u>eg;
<u>s</u>um, <u>j</u>ug, <u>b</u>us;
<u>s</u>ix, <u>p</u>ig, <u>l</u>ips.

**Page 8**

Row 1: book; row 2: tree; row 3: cat; row 4: house; row 5: bicycle.

**Page 9**

The teacher is under the table – no; The girl is reading a book – yes; The boy is painting the door – no; The teacher is looking at the girl – yes; The cat is reading a book – no; The boy has got a brush – yes; The hamster is on its cage – no.

**Page 12**

<u>c</u>lock, <u>b</u>ridge, <u>c</u>rown, <u>b</u>lack; <u>g</u>reen, <u>p</u>lug, <u>d</u>rill, <u>f</u>lag.

**Page 13**

sp: <u>sp</u>ider, <u>sp</u>oon, <u>sp</u>anner;
st: <u>st</u>ool, <u>st</u>amp, <u>st</u>ar;
sn: <u>sn</u>ail, <u>sn</u>ake, <u>sn</u>owman;
sw: <u>sw</u>an, <u>sw</u>itch, <u>sw</u>ing.

**Page 14**

cl – <u>c</u>lown, dr – <u>dr</u>um, sn – <u>sn</u>ail;
bl – <u>bl</u>ue, gr – <u>gr</u>apes;
sp – <u>sp</u>ider, st – <u>st</u>ar, sw – <u>sw</u>an.

**Page 16**

Everyone fell over and the turnip came out. **D**
The farmer saw an enormous turnip. **A**
Everyone tried to pull up the turnip. **C**
The farmer tried to pull up the turnip. **B**

**Page 18**

<u>b</u>all, <u>d</u>og, <u>c</u>at; b, c, d.
<u>h</u>ouse, <u>f</u>ish, <u>g</u>irl; f, g, h.
<u>l</u>adybird, <u>m</u>oon, <u>k</u>ey; k, l, m.
<u>r</u>abbit, <u>q</u>ueen, <u>p</u>arachute; p, q, r.
<u>u</u>mbrella, <u>s</u>eesaw, <u>t</u>elevision; s, t, u.

**Page 19**

or – f<u>or</u>k, us – b<u>us</u>, an – m<u>an</u>;
all – b<u>all</u>, am – l<u>am</u>b, in – tw<u>in</u>s;
at – b<u>at</u>.

**Page 20**

A little <u>girl</u> put on her dress.
The <u>sun</u> was hot.
I like getting into my <u>bed</u> to go to sleep.
I can see a bird's nest in the <u>tree</u>.
Dad kicked the <u>ball</u>.
A little <u>boy</u> put on his football boots.

**Page 21**

What is the time?
I like to eat fruit.
When do I go to school?
The car was going fast.
Who went up the hill with Jill?
The cat likes to sit on my lap.

There are 8 capital letters.

**Page 22**

Alison, Imran, Isabella, Jamilla, Meena, Oscar, Samuel, William.

**Page 23**

Wednesday, Saturday, Thursday, Friday, Sunday, Tuesday, Monday.

**Page 25**

9827, 9026, 9146, 9544.
Ms Walker, Mr Anderson, Mrs Todd, Mrs Depster.

**Page 26**

elephant: A large animal with a long trunk and ivory tusks. It lives in Africa and Asia.

kangaroo: A large animal that can jump very well. It carries its young in a pouch. It comes from Australia.

monkey: A small animal with long arms and feet that it uses like hands. It lives in jungles.

panda: A black and white animal like a bear. It lives in China.

zebra: An animal like a horse with black and white stripes. It lives in Africa.

**Page 27**

giraffes, penguins, whales, bears, turtles.
10, 4, 20, 18, 14.

**Page 28**

Things I eat: apple, banana, egg, grapes, sandwich.

Things I see on wheels: bicycle, bus, car, train, van.

**Page 29**

Things I use in the kitchen: food processor, frying pan, knife, pan, spoon.

Things I use in the garden: fork, lawnmower, spade, watering can, wheelbarrow.